Contents

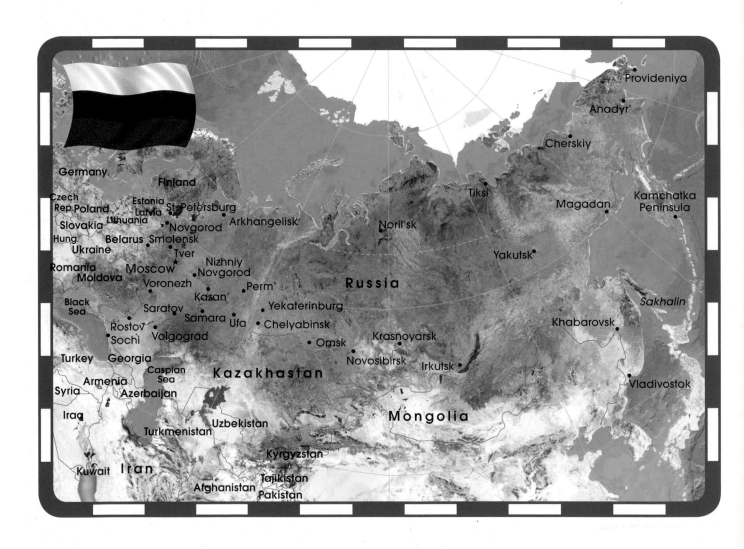

Travel Through Russia

Lynn Huggins-Cooper

QED Publishing

Copyright © QED Publishing 2007

First published in the UK in 2007 by
QED Publishing
A Quarto Group company
226 City Road
London EC1V 2TT

www.qed-publishing.co.uk

A Catalogue record for this book is available from the British Library.

ISBN 978 1 84538 756 3

Written by: Lynn Huggins-Cooper
Designed by: Rahul Dhiman (Q2A Media)
Editor: Honor Head
Picture Researcher: Sujatha Menon (Q2A Media)

Publisher Steve Evans
Creative Director Zeta Davies
Senior Editor Hannah Ray

Printed and bound in China

Picture credits

Key: t = top, b = bottom, c = centre,
l = left, r = right, FC = front cover

Dimitrios Kaisaris/ **Shutterstock**: 4t, **Index Stock Imagery**/ **Photolibrary**: 4, 13t, **Photo Researchers, Inc.**/ **Photolibrary**: 6t, 16b, **Peter Arnold Images Inc**/ **Photolibrary**: 6b, 26t, Lee Foster/ **Lonely Planet Images**: 7t, **Oxford Scientific Films**/ **Photolibrary**: 7b, Photolibrary.Com/ Photolibrary: 8t, Lexan | Dreamstime.com: 9t, Imagestate Ltd/ Photolibrary: 9b, Wolfgang Kaehler/**CORBIS**: 10b, Patrick Horton/ **Lonely Planet Images**: 11t, Jonathan Smith/ **Lonely Planet Images**: 11b, 19t, Martin Moos/ **Lonely Planet Images**: 12t, Denis Babenko/ **Shutterstock**: 12b, Ken Saigle/ **Istockphoto**: 14t, EML/ **Shutterstock**: 14b, elianet Ortiz/ **Istockphoto**: 15t, 17t, **Foodpix**/ **Photolibrary**: 18t, Alexei Novikov/ **Istockphoto**: 19b, Lystseva Marina/ITAR-TASS/**Corbis**: 20t, **Veer**/ **Photolibrary**: 20b, Kevin Hamm: 21b, Honza Soukup: 22t, **REUTERS**/Spare Spare : 23t, Jon Arnold Images/ Photolibrary: 23b, **Science Photo Library**/ **Photolibrary**: 24b, 25b, Robert Wallis/**Corbis**: 25t, **Picture Press**/ **Photolibrary**: 27t, Graham Bel/ **Lonely Planet Images**: 27b.

Words in **bold** can be found in the glossary on page 31.

Where in the world is Russia?

The Russian Federation is the largest country in the world. It covers an amazing one-eighth of the Earth's surface and spans eleven time zones. It has the eighth-biggest population in the world and is home to people from over 160 different **ethnic groups**. However, although it has a large population, Russia has a low **population density**. This is because the country covers such a vast area – there is a lot of space for people to live in. In fact, more than one-third of the country has less than one person per square kilometre. The weather gets very, very cold in many areas, and the living conditions are difficult. Most people in Russia live around the cities, such as Moscow, where the living conditions are easier.

Did you know?

OFFICIAL NAME: Russian Federation

LOCATION: Stretches from Europe across northern Asia

SURROUNDING COUNTRIES: Azerbaijan, Belarus, China, Estonia, Norway, Finland, Georgia, Kazakhstan, North Korea, Latvia, Lithuania, Mongolia, Norway, Poland, Ukraine

SURROUNDING SEAS AND OCEANS: Arctic Ocean, Baltic Sea, Barents Sea, Baring Sea, Black Sea, Caspian Sea, East Siberian Sea, Kara Sea, Laptev Sea, Pacific Ocean, Sea of Japan, Sea of Okhotsk

CAPITAL: Moscow

AREA: 17 075 200sq km

POPULATION: 143 million

LIFE EXPECTANCY: Male 60 years Female 74 years

RELIGIONS: **Russian Orthodox** (Christian), Islam

OFFICIAL LANGUAGE: Russian Written language – Cyrillic alphabet

CLIMATE: ranges from the Arctic north to the **temperate** south

HIGHEST MOUNTAIN: Mount El'brus (5642m high)

MAJOR RIVERS: Lena (4400km long)

Volga (3680km)

CURRENCY: rouble

What is Russia like?

Russia is a country of vast, sweeping landscapes. However, it is not all **rural**. The country has been through many changes and there are lots of wonderful historic buildings and monuments to see in beautiful cities such as Moscow and St Petersburg.

Coldest place on Earth

Russia is the coldest country in the world. Siberia, which makes up over half of the area of Russia, is the coldest part of the country but 40 million people still live there. Parts of Siberia are actually colder than the North Pole, and the far north is covered in snow all the time. However, as Russia is such a large country, the climate does vary. As you travel to the area around the Black Sea, there are seaside resorts such as Sochi, Anapa and Gelendzhik, where the weather is warm and the water temperature reaches up to 26°C.

In the Taymyr Peninsula, in Northern Siberia, it can be extremely cold and the living conditions are hard, but 39 000 people still live there.

The Urals have rich deposits of gold and gemstones, such as topaz. These can sometimes be found exposed on the ground where the soil and rock have been worn away by the weather.

Russia has many impressive monuments, such as the Narva Triumphal Arch in St Petersburg.

Women workers

More than 50 per cent of Russia's workforce is female. This may be because there are many more women than men in Russia. Most trams, buses, and railways are run by women. Other professions such as medicine, dentistry and teaching are also dominated by women.

Changing landscapes

Russia covers a huge area, and has many different types of landscape. There are mountainous regions such as the Urals, which run in a line from north to south, separating European and Asian Russia. There are also huge, ancient **coniferous** forests called **taiga**. In Siberia, there are large areas of **tundra**. Tundra is an area where the **subsoil** is permanently frozen (known as permafrost) and there are no trees. Only mosses, lichen and grasses can grow there. In the winter, the ground is frozen solid. In the summer, the topsoil thaws and becomes very wet, with many marshes, lakes, **bogs** and streams. In European Russia, there are huge **plains**, which are called the **steppes**. These are grasslands, and are used for farming.

Many animals live in the Russian taiga, including squirrels, foxes, elks, wolverines and the endangered Siberian crane.

History of Russia

From 1547, Russia was ruled by **Tsars** (who were like emperors or kings). People were born into the ruling family in the same way as they still are in countries such as the United Kingdom. The Tsars were very rich and lived in fabulous palaces.

Nicholas II was Tsar of Russia from 1894 – 1917. This picture shows him with his son, Alexis, in 1911.

The last Tsar

The last Tsar to rule in Russia was Nicholas II. At the time of his rule, many Russian people were very poor. There were terrible food shortages and many people were starving. The Russian army had suffered terrible losses during the First World War. They had not been sent enough supplies of food or weapons. People were sick of being treated badly. In 1917, the people rose up, overthrew the Tsars and took over the country in the Russian Revolution. In February 1917, Tsar Nicholas II gave up his throne and the Provisional Government was created.

In 1918, Tsar Nicholas II and his family were executed. Some people believe that one of his daughters, Anastasia, escaped, but this has never been proven.

Lenin, the Bolsheviks and civil war

The Provisional Government was not in power for very long. In October 1917, it was overthrown by the **Bolsheviks**, led by Vladimir Lenin. In 1918, civil war broke out in Russia between the Bolshevik Red Army (the Communists) and the White Army (the monarchists). The Communists did not want Tsars to rule and wanted the people to have more power. The monarchists believed there should still be Tsars ruling Russia. Millions of people died before the war ended in 1921. The Communist Red Army won after three years of hard fighting.

Lenin became one of the most famous revolutionaries of the 20th century. Many statues were erected in his honour, such as this one in Vologda.

During the Russian Revolution many posters were produced to encourage the people to rise up against the enemy.

The USSR

In 1922, the Union of Soviet Socialist Republics (USSR) was created. It was a socialist state. That means that there was no private property, belonging to a few rich people. This was supposed to make things fair for the workers, who would have some control over their work and lives. The USSR existed until 1991. In 1991, the USSR was dissolved and the Russian Federation was created. Its first leader was Boris Yeltsin.

Getting about

The railway is one of the main ways of travelling in Russia as many of the roads are quite poor. There are 87 079km of railway track in Russia, which has the largest and busiest rail network in the world.

The Trans-Siberian Express

The Trans-Siberian Express is one of the best ways of seeing Russia. You can travel all the way from Moscow, in the far west of the country, to Vladivostok on the east coast. From here you can take the ferry on to Yokohama in Japan. The journey from Moscow to Yokohama takes ten days in total and there are sleeping compartments on the train. The journey crosses seven time zones and 9745km.

When the Trans-Siberian Railway was built in the 1890s, Russian engineers started to build at both ends and met in the middle.

The Trans-Mongolian Railway

The Trans-Mongolian Railway takes passengers to Beijing, in China. It runs from Moscow to Irkutsk, one of the largest cities in Siberia. From here, it travels near Lake Baikal, the world's largest freshwater lake, before travelling on into Mongolia and finally on to China and Beijing. The journey covers 9344km and takes six days.

There are restaurant cars on every train on the Trans-Siberian and Trans-Mongolian Railways.

Over nine million people use the Moscow Metro every day.

Kievskaya station on the Moscow Metro is very ornate, with many beautiful mosaics.

✉ YOU'VE GOT MAIL

The long distance trains in Russia are great but so is the underground train system in Moscow. The Moscow Metro has unbelievable stations – they are so beautiful you'd think you had stumbled into a museum or palace! The stations began to be built in 1935. They were meant to show off Soviet architecture and design and were often called 'Peoples' Palaces.' Some stations even have marble walls and sparkling chandeliers!

Ivan

Sites to see

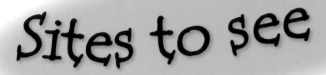

As you journey through Russia, there are many wonderful things to see, both from the time of the Tsars and from the Communist era.

Architecture

No trip to Russia would be complete without a visit to Moscow's Red Square and the Kremlin, which is the beautiful building where the Russian president lives. Many of the buildings around Red Square look as though they are from a fairytale. The Cathedral of the Assumption, built in the 1470s, has stunning golden domes and the Church of St Basil the Blessed, on the edge of Red Square, has eight onion-shaped, dome-topped towers arranged around a central, ninth spire.

The Hermitage

The Hermitage in St Petersburg is one of the world's largest museums. There are over three million objects on display. The building itself is very beautiful. It is also called the Winter Palace and was once the main residence of the Tsars. As you wander around the building, you can see marble staircases, golden ceilings, crystal chandeliers and fabulous **mosaic** work. You can also visit the Gold Rooms which house a collection of priceless royal jewels.

The stunning Hermitage has over 40 000 drawings, 8000 paintings and 500 000 engravings amongst its exhibits.

St Basil's Cathedral was built between 1555 and 1561. Its beautiful coloured domes are a landmark in Moscow.

The Kremlin wall is 2235m long, and in places it is an amazing 19m tall! It was originally built as a defence against invaders.

Today we went to Red Square, in the centre of Moscow. It is huge! I remembered looking at photos in my history books at school of the Communist parades they used to hold here. The most famous of these parades were the annual parades on May Day – a national holiday to celebrate the working people of the Soviet Union. The Soviet military used to march through the square in front of the Communist leaders – it was a good way of showing off Russia's military power! It is thought that Red Square got its name in the seventeenth century, because the Russian word 'krasnaya', which was used to describe nearby St Basil's Cathedral, can mean 'beautiful' or 'red'. The name spread to include the area of the square, as well as the cathedral. These days, the square is often used for pop concerts. I saw a display of photos that showed the square full of people watching the Russian Live 8 pop concert in 2005, which was all about fighting against world poverty.

Anna

Art in Russia

Russia is full of wonderful types of art, from ballet and music to beautiful craftwork, such as nesting Russian dolls and **lacquer** work.

Making music

Some of the best composers in the world came from Russia, such as Rimsky-Korsakov, Prokofiev, Rachmaninoff and Shostakovich. People all over the world enjoy listening to classical music written by Russian composers. Today, many Russian people also enjoy rock concerts by bands who play heavy-metal music to huge crowds in venues such as Red Square.

Russian dolls stack inside one another, getting smaller and smaller each time.

Russian ballet companies tour all over the world.

Dolls in dolls

Under Communist rule in Russia, people were not allowed to worship God, so **icon** painters were not allowed to paint and sell icons. Instead, they made lacquer boxes, often decorated with pictures of Russian fairytales. They also made the famous Russian dolls, or matryoshka. The word matryoshka comes from the latin word 'mater' which means mother.

The beautiful eggs made by Fabergé were often decorated with precious jewels or semi-precious stones.

Fabulous Fabergé

In the 1880s, a jeweller called Fabergé made egg-shaped boxes from gold and silver. These were given by the Tsars as presents at Easter. The top half of the eggs opened and inside were tiny surprises such as a carriage made from gold. Today, collectors pay lots of money for the eggs. In 1913, Tsar Nicholas II had *The Winter Egg* made as a gift for his mother. In 1994, it sold at auction for $5.5 million!

Breathtaking ballet

Some of the best ballet companies in the world are based in Russia such as the Bolshoi in Moscow and the Kirov in St Petersburg. The famous ballet dancer Nureyev used to dance for the Bolshoi. These ballet companies tour all over the world, performing both classical and modern ballet, but if you visit Russia, a trip to the ballet is a real treat.

As a special treat, my mum took me to the ballet to see The Nutcracker. It tells the story of a girl who is given a magical nutcracker, which comes to life as a prince and battles the evil Rat King. The dancers were like beautiful princesses but the Rat King was terrifying! He was a great dancer and made lots of huge leaps into the air, waving his sword at the poor nutcracker-prince.
Katya

Farming in Russia

As you travel across Russia, you will see huge areas of farmland. In the colder, northern parts of the country, the fields are full of wheat, corn, flax, hemp, millet, rice and potatoes. In some southern regions, it is warm enough to grow citrus fruits. Lots of apples, pears and cherries are also grown. There is an especially **fertile** triangle of land from St Petersburg and Ukraine in the west to southern Siberia in the east. Many crops are grown here.

Crops

Russia is the world's leading producer of potatoes, barley, rye and oats. It is the world's third-biggest producer of wheat. In the early 1990s, Russia grew 46 million tonnes of wheat, 25.5 million tonnes of barley, 13.9 million tonnes of rye and 11.5 million tonnes of oats every year!

I have been finding out about the Nenets, a group of people who live in the far north of Siberia. They are reindeer herders. Their herds of reindeer provide them with food, clothing and the raw material to make their houses – tents called chooms that are made from reindeer skins. The Nenets are nomads, which means they move from one place to another when the season changes, pulling their belongings along on wooden sleds. It is a very hard life.
Leon

The Nenets' herding dogs are very intelligent. They herd the reindeer and then help to guard them.

Fishing

Russia has one of the largest fishing industries in the world. Most fish caught are **marine** fish, but many fish are also caught in freshwater lakes and rivers. These include salmon, sturgeon, oilfish, pike and perch.

Farm animals

Cattle are the most common form of **livestock** in Russia. Sheep and goats are also kept on many farms. Pigs are farmed in parts of European Russia, and grain, potatoes and sugar beets are grown as animal fodder. However, not many chickens are farmed, because frozen chicken is **imported** very cheaply from countries such as the United States. Frozen chicken meat is one of Russia's largest import items.

Russia provides one-fourth of the world's fresh and frozen fish.

Cattle have been farmed in the Caucasus region of Russia for hundreds of years.

Food and drink

The **staple diet** in Russia is made up of grain, potatoes, oil and sugar. Russia sometimes has food shortages and fresh fruits and vegetables can be a luxury. However, this is changing and many people now grow their own vegetables.

Borscht is made from beetroot and often has lemon and sugar added just before serving to make it taste sweet.

In Russia, herring mixed with potato, carrot, beetroot and mayonnaise is called seledka pod shuboy, which means 'herring in a sheepskin coat'!

Traditional dishes

There are many wonderful foods cooked and eaten in Russia. You can try borscht – cold beetroot soup which looks beautiful in the bowl as it is a deep, ruby-red colour. It is served with a blob of soured cream. As you journey through Russia, you should try blinis. These are small pancakes and are eaten served with a dollop of **crème fraîche** and caviar – fish eggs!

Shashliki are similar to kebabs. The meat is cooked on skewers over a barbecue.

Pirozhki can also be stuffed with fruit, to make a sweet version. The word pirozhki means 'little pies'.

Black bread and meat

Shashliki is a meat dish, often made with chicken or lamb. The meat is soaked in vinegar and water and then grilled over a fire. It is sometimes eaten with special black bread. Black bread is made from rye and is quite hard. It is eaten all over Russia and is very tasty.

Pick a pie

Small meat or vegetable pastries called pirozhki are very popular in Russia. They are eaten hot or cold and they are often on sale from stalls in the street. Fish is also very popular. Sea bass, trout and a fish called siomga are sliced very thinly and served with slices of lemon.

One of my favourite foods is syrniki. These are like patties or burgers made from tvorog – a sort of soft cheese, a little like cottage cheese. They are fried and eaten with honey or jam. I also love to drink sbiten, a lovely, hot drink made from honey and spices.
Elena

Festivals and holidays

Many festivals are celebrated in Russia, with music, dancing, parades and fireworks. Some festivals are religious, such as Christmas, but others are left over from Soviet Russia, such as International Women's Day.

Christmas

On 7 January, many Russians celebrate the Russian Orthodox Christmas. Christmas was banned in Russia after the 1917 revolution, and was not celebrated during the whole time that Russia was a Communist state. That does not mean there were no winter celebrations though! New Year's celebrations were held that were similar to a lot of Christmas celebrations. Grandfather Frost (known as Ded Moroz in Russian) used to visit children and bring presents, just like Father Christmas. Christmas was reintroduced in 1992, when the Russian Federation was created.

To celebrate New Year, fireworks go off over St Basil's Cathedral, in Red Square.

Christmas fairs are very popular in Russia. Gorgeous baubles are sold, to be hung on Christmas trees.

Special day

International Women's Day is celebrated on 8 March. On this day, people remember all the incredible women who have helped to make the world a better place to live in and have fought for the rights of women. Today, International Women's Day is celebrated around the world but it started in Russia, where women are given special treats. It is a bit like Mothering Sunday in western Europe, but all women are celebrated – not just mothers.

At Christmas, we plan to visit some friends in St Petersburg! Dad says we will go to church on Christmas Eve and then have a twelve-course supper including fish, borscht, cabbage stuffed with millet, cooked dried fruit and lots more! Mum told me the Russian story about a little peasant woman called Babushka. Apparently, she missed seeing the baby Jesus on his journey to Bethlehem so she leaves presents for all children now, so that she will never miss him again. With luck, my brother and I will get a present from her! We shall open our family presents on Christmas Day, as usual. Then we have another big meal and a party. It will be such fun! What do you do for Christmas?
love
Olga

These people are putting the finishing touches to a Christmas tree in the Russian city of Kolpino.

Two cities

Special sheeting is used to protect the pitch from harsh winter weather.

Russia has many beautiful cities for visitors to enjoy, but two of the most famous are Moscow and St Petersburg.

Smolny cathedral is a beautiful building that is part of the complex built to house the Smolny Boarding School.

City of Tsars

St Petersburg was also known as the City of Tsars. This is because it is where the Tsars lived, along with the rest of the Imperial Russian family, in the Hermitage. As you wander through the wide and elegant avenues of St Petersburg, you can imagine how it was in the time of the Tsars. Apart from the Hermitage, you can visit the Russian Museum, the Mikhailovsky Castle and the Summer Garden. The Mikhailovsky Castle was built for Emperor Paul I, and was supposed to be very safe. Unfortunately it was not safe enough – the emperor was assassinated in his own bedroom on 12 March, 1801, shortly after he moved into his new home. The Summer Garden was built by Tsar Peter the Great in 1704. It is a very beautiful park filled with statues, fountains and rare plants.

Revolutionary headquarters

In St Petersburg, you should also visit the Smolny Boarding School for Young Ladies of Noble Birth which was built in 1806. It is a beautiful building but also interesting because, during the Russian Revolution, the school became the headquarters of the Bolsheviks. Lenin, the leader of the Bolsheviks, lived at Smolny during the revolution.

Peter the Great became Tsar of Russia when he was only 10 years old.

Moscow

The capital of Russia, Moscow, is on the banks of the River Moskva, in the European part of Russia. It has lots of interesting historic buildings to visit, such as the Kremlin, and modern structures, such as the Federation Tower. There are also lots of cafes and restaurants around the main street, Tverskaya Street, and many shops. Moscow is also a centre for Russian performing arts, such as ballet and film.

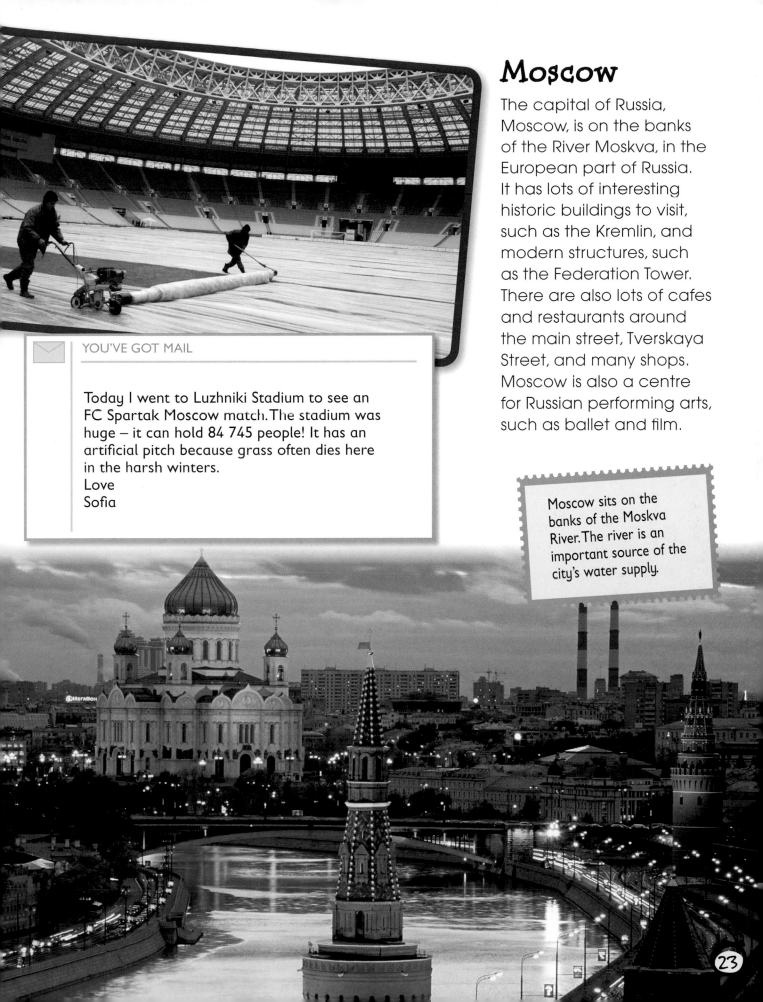

YOU'VE GOT MAIL

Today I went to Luzhniki Stadium to see an FC Spartak Moscow match. The stadium was huge – it can hold 84 745 people! It has an artificial pitch because grass often dies here in the harsh winters.
Love
Sofia

Moscow sits on the banks of the Moskva River. The river is an important source of the city's water supply.

Russian exports

Russia **exports** goods all over the world. Siberia contains a third of the world's supplies of natural gas and it is sold to many different countries. Russia also exports wood, machinery, chemicals, military equipment, gold, diamonds, metals, coal and oil. Siberia produces 8.4 million barrels of oil a day!

Flax exports

Russia also exports cereals and other agricultural crops around the world. Flax, which is used to create **textiles** and oil, will grow in cold temperatures and poor soils and has been planted in large areas. Russia produced about half of the world's flax crop in the 1980s.

Diamond mining is the main industry in the Sakha area of Russia.

Workers come from all over the world to work in the Siberian oilfields.

Most gold mining takes place in the far east of Russia. Russia is the fifth-largest producer of gold in the world.

YOU'VE GOT MAIL

We went on a tour of the Mir diamond mine, in Mirny in east Siberia. It is an open-cast mine, and looks like a huge hole in the ground. Massive machines were used to cut the diamonds out of the earth. Mir is one of the deepest open-cast mines in the world. It takes a truck nearly two hours to drive from the bottom of the mine to its rim!

We also visited the diamond-processing factory and saw some stones worth lots of money. We found out that diamond is a mineral made from pure carbon – just like the black graphite used in pencils and even ordinary soot! It was incredible to think that the rough stones we saw would become shining jewels once they were cut. We were told that diamond is the hardest natural substance on Earth. It can only be cut or polished by another diamond. It was wonderful to see the beautifully cut stones.

Alexander

The environment

Russia has a big problem with the amount of pollution from the huge industrial and chemical plants that were built during the time of the Soviet Union. Many of these factories are still in use but they are very old and need updating.

Lake Baikal is home to the world's only freshwater seal. It is called the nerpa by local people.

Deepest lake

Lake Baikal, often called the 'Blue eye of Siberia' is the deepest lake in the world. Discharge from the chemical industry is polluting its waters. Cutting down logs is also creating problems as chemicals such as herbicides are sprayed on plants to kill them. These chemicals get into the lake water and kill water creatures. There is a major campaign to protect this unique habitat.

Local legend says that if you swim in the freezing-cold Lake Baikal, you will add 20 years to your life.

Today we went to Lake Baikal – it's huge! There are over fifty species of fish in the clear water and there's lots of wildlife that lives around the lake, including brown bears, elk, moose and deer. Dad wanted to take some wildlife photos and he got a great one of a bear catching fish. There are loads of rocky islands on the lake. Apparently, the biggest one, Olkhon Island, was the birthplace of the fierce Mongolian ruler Genghis Khan!

Dmitry

New lakes, lost lakes

Global warming is changing the landscape of Siberia. Permafrost exists all over the world, but Russia has the most, covering more than 10 million square kilometres. As temperatures rise, the permafrost is melting. As it melts, carbon and methane are released into the air, which contribute to global warming and make the problem worse. New lakes are forming in the north and existing lakes are growing. Some buildings and houses built upon the permafrost are **subsiding**. In the south, lakes are disappearing completely as the permafrost breaks down and water seeps deep into the ground. All of these changes affect wildlife.

Activity ideas

1 Using travel brochures and websites, find the images and pictures of Russia most often shown to tourists travelling to the country. Print out the pictures to make a collage of 'Tourist Russia'. What are the most popular tourist destinations in Russia? What ideas and images do travel websites use to sell Russia as a place to go on holiday?

2 Find a recipe for borscht in a recipe book or on the Internet. With an adult, buy the ingredients and make it! What do you think of it?

NOTE FOR ADULTS: Please ensure that children do not suffer from any food allergies before making or eating any food.

3 Where would you like to visit most in Russia? Design and write a postcard from your dream holiday destination.

4 Using books and the Internet, find out about Lake Baikal. Make a fact file about the lake and the creatures who live in and around it. Draw or print out pictures to add to your fact file.

5 Imagine you are travelling through Russia on the Trans-Siberian Express. What can you see from the window? Write a diary entry about your journey.

6 Make your own Fabergé egg. Ask an adult to help you to blow an egg. Once you have washed the empty egg shell, use PVA glue to cover it in layers of tissue paper. Add sequins and plastic jewels to decorate your own precious egg.

7 Look up the Russian cyrillic alphabet online. Can you work out how to write your name? Make a plaque for your bedroom door, with your name written in Russian.

8 Find recordings of music written by Russian composers such as Shostakovich. While you are listening, paint a picture or write a story to go with the music.

10 Using an atlas, find other places on the same **latitude** as Siberia. Find out if the average temperatures are the same, or if they differ. Plot the temperatures of the different places on a graph. Do any people live in the other places you have found out about?

9 Find out more about International Women's Day. When was it first celebrated in Russia? Write a report about the ways people celebrate.

12 Using your school library and the Internet, do some more research on the taiga. How much land does it cover? Does anybody live there? Which animals live there? Find out if any other countries have areas of taiga.

11 Using three plastic bottles of different sizes, make a model of some Russian dolls. (Make sure they fit inside each other!) Cut the bottom off each bottle. Tear strips of newspaper and cover each of your bottles in a thin layer of papier mâché. When the papier mâché is dry, paint clothes and faces onto your dolls. When they are dry, cover them in a layer of PVA glue. It will look messy at first but dries clear and will protect your models.

13 With an adult, buy some rye bread. (You can buy it at the supermarket or from health food shops.) Taste the bread and compare it to white bread, made with wheat. Talk about taste, texture and appearance. Which do you prefer?

NOTE FOR ADULTS: Please ensure that children do not suffer from any food allergies before making or eating any food.

14 Carry out research using the Internet, magazines and newspapers to find out more about the problem of global warming, and the effects it is having upon the Siberian permafrost. Use the information you find to design a poster to tell people about the dangers to the environment.

15 Find out about a story from a Russian ballet. Listen to the music, and then design a stage set for the ballet. You could design costumes for the dancers, too.

17 Choose one of the famous buildings in Russia that tourists like to visit. Pretend you are a tour guide. Research the building and then write a talk you could give to a group you were showing around.

16 See if you can discover more about how diamonds are mined, and how the rough stones are made into sparkling jewels. Write down the process as a flow-chart.

19 Find a Russian fairytale from a book or the Internet. Make a comic strip of the story. Remember, you need to tell as much of the story as possible with pictures as there is not room for many words!

18 Write a leaflet for tourists describing the Kremlin. Describe the place using language that will encourage people to visit.

20 Make a 3D map of Russia using papier mâché. Draw the rough shape on a sheet of card, and add pieces of crumpled paper, glued firmly in place, to build up the land. Coat the model in PVA glue, and cover the whole model carefully with a strips of tissue paper. Repeat this step until you have a smooth surface and leave to dry. Then paint and label your model with major cities, rivers, mountains and areas of taiga and tundra.

Glossary

bog An area of soft, muddy, waterlogged ground

Bolsheviks Members of the Russian Social Democratic Workers' Party that seized power in Russia in October 1917

coniferous Evergreen, such as spruce or fir trees

crème fraîche Creamy, thick dairy product, a bit like yoghurt

ethnic groups A group of people who identify with each other, usually because of a shared ancestry. People within an ethnic group often speak the same language and have similar customs

exports Goods sent out of the country to be sold in other countries

fertile Soil that is rich is goodness. Crops grow well in fertile soil

icons A picture or object that represents someone or something of religious importance

imported When goods have been brought into the country from other countries

lacquer A hard, glossy coating

latitude Distance from the equator (an imaginary circle around the middle of the earth, shown on most maps)

livestock Animals kept on a farm

marine From the sea

mosaic Patterns and pictures made from lots of tiny tiles

plains Flat, open areas of land

population density The number of people living in a certain amount of land. If there are a lot of people, the place has a high population density

rural In the countryside

Russian Orthodox Main Christian Church found in Russia

staple diet What people eat on a regular basis; the foods eaten regularly

steppes Dry, grass-covered plain

subsiding Sinking into the ground

subsoil The layer of soil that lies beneath the topsoil (which is the layer of soil on the surface)

taiga Coniferous forests found in sub-arctic regions

temperate When the weather is never very hot nor very cold

textiles Fabrics

tundra Treeless plains found in the arctic regions

Tsar Ruler of Russia before the Russian revolution

Index